Hibbert Lectures, 1923

A LIVING UNIVERSE

L. P. JACKS, D.D., LL.D., D.Litt.

A LIVING UNIVERSE

Three Lectures

BY

L. P. JACKS, D.D., LL.D., D.Litt.

PRINCIPAL OF MANCHESTER COLLEGE, OXFORD

*Author of "The Legends of Smokeover," "Religious
Perplexities," "Realities and Shams," etc.*

NEW YORK
GEORGE H. DORAN COMPANY

A LIVING UNIVERSE
— A —
PRINTED IN THE UNITED STATES OF AMERICA

FOREWORD

In presenting these lectures in the form of a book, I have adopted a different plan from that which seemed best in my former volume, *Religious Perplexities*. For reasons connected with the nature of the subject matter I found it necessary, in that volume, to revise the spoken form throughout. But here, the subject being different, I have thought it better to keep my audience still before me. I find, however, on consulting my record of the lectures, which is an ample one, that in actual delivery I varied them considerably, enlarging now upon one point, now upon another, according to my audience, the character of which differed in the four cities to which I was sent by the Hibbert Trustees. The consequence is that a reader who happens to have heard the lectures in any of those cities will find in the book more than he heard on certain points and less than he heard on others. But I wish not to lose the sense that I am still addressing him. By altering the spoken form, I might indeed have produced a more closely knitted fabric and avoided some offence to the literary graces; but I should have done less justice to my own feeling of the urgency of the topic.

The first two lectures were delivered, at the instance of the Hibbert Trustees, in Sheffield, Newcastle-on-Tyne, Edinburgh and London, in April and May 1923. The third, which I am permitted to include with the two Hibbert Lectures, was given in Oxford to University Extension students in August. It rounds off my thoughts about a Living Universe.

L. P. J.

CONTENTS

I: EDUCATION AND RELIGION IN A LIVING UNIVERSE

I: Education and Religion in a Living Universe

I HAVE never yet been able to find a definition of "education" which I could offer to an audience as satisfactory to myself or likely to prove satisfactory to others. Most of the definitions I have come across—and there have been a good many—make use of terms that are more difficult to define than "education" itself.

According to one definition education is "preparation for life." But what is "life"? The disagreements on that point are wide and deep. And if we don't agree as to the meaning of life how can we agree as to the right method of preparing for it?

Another definition very popular just now declares that education is "the training of good citizens." But what is a good citizen? A person who would be a good citizen in one kind of State or one kind of city might be a bad citizen in another kind. Before you can define a

good citizen you have to define the kind of city
or State you want him to live in—and that
is not an easy matter.

Men differ endlessly in their notions of what
a good citizen is, and these differences will be
reflected and repeated when they come to the
question of training him. The Bolshevists in
Russia are at this moment busy in setting up
schools for the training of good citizens—in
their sense of the term. But before we can
accept these schools as models for education
we must accept the Bolshevist notion of the
State—which some of us are not yet willing
to do. And so in general, when people speak
of a good citizen they generally have in their
thoughts a person more or less resembling
themselves. The official mind at Whitehall is
willing enough to accept the formula that education is the training of a good citizen. But
the good citizen Whitehall is thinking of is always the kind of person who would keep Whitehall in existence. A person who proposed to
sweep away the whole official system, and the
salaries dependent upon it, would be a bad citizen according to the official mind, and we could
hardly expect Whitehall to take a hand in

training him, and to vote public money for his training.

These are some of the difficulties we fall into when we define education. Our definitions are useful up to a point, but when we come to their actual applications they break down and give us no further guidance.

Nevertheless I recommend the defining of education as a profitable exercise for private meditation. Let each of us ask himself what he means by "education" and ponder the question in the solitude of his chamber. We shall then realise what a tremendous question we have raised. We shall find that in order to answer it we have to probe down to the innermost meaning of the universe itself. Problems which have exercised the greatest philosophers will rise up before us. In particular we shall find ourselves asking the question—Is the universe dead or alive?—and unable to define education until we have settled that. We shall see that the kind of education suitable for man in a dead universe would be unsuitable for him in a living one.

Thinking about education compels us to face these big questions; and that is why thinking about it is so good for us all. If you want a man to think deeply and earnestly, and with the fear of God upon him, set him thinking about education. He will soon find out, for example, that religion and education are not two things, but one thing; two only on the surface, but one in the ultimate foundations and the final aim. Not two things that can say to one another: "You go your way and I will go mine," but things that must move together and move in the same direction if they are to move to good ends. There is nothing like education for turning the plain man into a thinker. It will get him earnest, it will bring him up against reality, in half the time that would be taken if he began his thinking on the stock conundrums of the philosopher, or on the questions that are debated among the sects. Get him thinking about education, if you want him to make discoveries. More people are thinking about it today than ever thought about it before. It is a hopeful sign of the times. Something will come of that.

All that is for your private meditation, I ask you to define education for yourselves. The effort, believe me, will not be wasted. I have

myself learnt things by trying to define education which I could never have learnt in any
other way, and I believe the same would happen
to everybody. I read lately that there are two
classes of people in the world. There are the
people who can only learn what they are taught
by somebody else; and there are the people who
are incessantly learning for themselves. The
latter is the more promising class, and it is in-
creasing at the present day. Perhaps the most
portentous phenomenon of our times is the
rapid increase of the class who are no longer
dependent on what they are taught by others,
but are beginning to teach themselves. Let
each of us learn for himself what education is.
Depend upon it he will learn many other things
at the same time.

Instead, therefore, of defining education, I
am going to attempt something else. What
most of us need at the moment is not so much
a new definition of education as a new *vision*
of it. Visions are more potent things than definitions. Our existing vision of education is
cramped, limited, narrow and altogether inade-
quate to the full compass and reality of the
thing we are talking about.

Reality, Religion and Education seem to me to form an indivisible unity. Take them apart and all three will be misunderstood. Each of them needs the light that is thrown upon it by the other two.

First as to Religion and Education. It is of the utmost importance that educationists and religious teachers, schoolmasters and clergymen, should think of themselves as co-operators in a common task. That all education should be religious we have often been told. It is equally true that all religion should be educational—a point that is sometimes overlooked. The two should form a partnership and there should be no attempt at domination on either side. In the new age that is dawning for both of them they will need each other's help. Education will have much to learn from religion: but religion also will have much to learn from education. On the one hand, a religious spirit must enter into education; on the other, an educational spirit must enter into religion. This last must not be forgotten.

Education is commonly classified under three heads—primary, secondary, and higher. To these three I should like to add a fourth, *highest*

—primary, secondary, higher and highest. The highest education is religion. It needs to be prepared for by the three kinds which precede it. That which begins as primary education should end in religion. That which ends as religion should begin in primary education. Religion might be defined as education raised to its highest power.

In the Epistle to the Hebrews it is said of Christ that He learnt obedience through the things that He suffered—a remarkable saying, which reminds us that He was a learner as well as a teacher, as all true teachers must needs be. The education of this great spirit went on; it went on through suffering until it reached its climax in what we know. That which began in the carpenter's shop ended on Calvary and the Cross—the highest education linked by an unbroken chain to those primary and elemental lessons which a child may learn in playing with his father's tools, or in watching a man at work. So in all that I have to say about education I shall not be speaking of a short-lived process which ends when the school or the university is left behind. I shall be speaking of a life-long process, the largest part of which comes neither from the school nor from the university, but from the general work of life. When education is thought of in that way it is not easily distinguished from religion.

In the best educational practice of the day the watchword is continuity. Time was when the three kinds of education were regarded as distinct and independent—primary for the poor, secondary for the middle class, higher for the rich—a dismal and disastrous theory. Nobody who understands what he is about would hold such a view to-day. All hinges on continuity. The function of primary education is to lead on to secondary, and of secondary to lead on to higher. And the function of all three together is to lead on to that highest education which comes from a faithful performance of the work of life, and to that very highest which teaches men obedience through the things they suffer —the lesson of the Cross. All is continuous; all is of one piece; and there is no stage of it which can do its work efficiently unless it looks forward to the stages that come after and backward to the stages that went before. That is why I would have education and religion linked together. The two are indivisibly one, and you

can have no reality in either unless you have
reality in the other.

All this can be put in the language of fact.
To-day there are in this country about seven
million young people passing through the three
forms of education—primary, secondary, and
higher. Take a few years of that and you have
the whole community as it will be in the next
generation. Now ask this question: If that
goes wrong, what else is likely to go right?
If the battle of civilisation is lost in the schools,
who is going to win it afterwards? If the
whole community is set wrong in its education,
what chances have the clergy of being able to
set it right from the pulpit? What are the
chances of legislation? To begin by starting
the community on the wrong road, in the plas-
tic period, and then, when it is grown up, to
send out the parson and the policeman to bring
it back—what fool's enterprise could compare
with that?

Indeed I might have asked at once—What
are the chances for the Community of Nations
unless the basis for it is laid in education?
What is the use of drawing up international
compacts of peace and goodwill if the seeds of

peace and goodwill have never been sown in the hearts of the rising generation? Such compacts can be *made*—that is relatively easy—but unless education supports them they will never be *kept*.

However, I must leave all that aside, to be dealt with more fully in my second lecture. Enough for the moment if we think of religion and education as forming an indivisible unity. Take them apart, think of them as separate, and both will suffer damage. Religion will be a thing for which there has been no preparation: education will be a process that leads on to no definite goal. The realities of the one are the realities of the other.

What, then, do I mean by reality? To answer that is not so easy.

The poet Goethe has a saying that can help us. "The highest cannot be spoken." I think it profoundly true. But at first sight it looks like a disability. It would seem that the highest must always escape us, because we cannot *speak* it, and so communicate it one to another. But that is a mistake.

Though the highest <u>cannot</u> be *spoken,* <u>it can always be *acted*</u>. By *acting* it, we not only

grasp it firmly ourselves, but we communicate
it in the clearest manner one to another.   There
is a language of action as well as a language of
words; and of the two the language of action
is the more telling, the more intelligible, the
more unmistakable, and in the deepest sense the
more eloquent.   Some of the profoundest truths
ever revealed to mankind have been conveyed
through the language of action.   Christianity
is an example.   The language of words always
halts behind the inner secret of that religion,
and half says what only a Christian deed can
fully express.   The language of words is a
wonderful instrument—I should get on very
badly without it in this lecture—but there are
some things it cannot do.   As an instrument
for the expression of the highest it is inade-
quate.

Now what are these "highest" things that
cannot be spoken?   They are the ultimate realities of the universe.   God is the chief of them,
the summary of them all.   In the deepest sense,
not one of them is speakable.   But all are actable.   Were we dependent on speech alone they
would be unknowables.   But because we can
act them, we may not only know them ourselves,

Language of action.

actions transcend words.

Highest things —

but make them known to others. No man can fully *say* what he means by God. But every man can act what he means. God, you say, is Love. Yes: but nobody will know what you mean by *saying* that God is Love unless you *act* it as well. Neither will you know yourself. Reality, then, though not fully speakable, is actable, and there is no disability to be lamented.

The word "actable" may not altogether please you. It may suggest play-acting, the theatre and the stage, and all that world of unreality—not a word to use, therefore, when we are trying to understand what reality is. I will say something about that, for it bears on my subject.

Play-acting, of course, is often a frivolous affair. But in the hands of a great master, like Sophocles or Shakespeare, there is nothing more serious under the sun. I rank the drama, when a great master is handling it, as one of the most powerful instruments ever invented for conveying the highest truths to the human mind. The truths that it conveys are of a kind that could be conveyed in no other way. Have you never felt, after witnessing a fine performance of *Othello* or of *Lear,* that something has been shown you which you cannot put into words, but which you recognise as profoundly and tremendously true? Who can *say* exactly what it means when Othello slays Desdemona, or when Cordelia dies in the arms of her distracted father? But who does not *know* what it means when he sees it in action? At such times we catch the truth of Goethe's saying—"The highest cannot be spoken." None the less, it can be acted, and become through the action perfectly convincing to those for whom it is meant. Again I refer you to Christianity. Take out of Christianity the acted part, and leave only the spoken part, and what would that be worth? What would become of the *power* if the action were left out? What would become of the highest truth? <u>It is not the preaching but the thing preached about that *tells* in Christianity</u>. And <u>that is the *deed*</u>. Is not Christianity a divine drama—the greatest that has ever been staged on the world's history? Do not its truth, its power, its reality pivot on a deed that is done? "Go thou and *do* likewise."

Deeds

But here you will remind me that errors as well as truths can be acted. So indeed they can. Nay more. The worst things in this world resemble the best things in being actable but unspeakable.   Nevertheless there is a difference.

When the worst things are acted upon the stage of history, whether by individuals or by nations, you will observe that the drama, after reaching a certain point, ceases to be a drama, loses unity and meaning, and breaks up into nonsensical confusion, like the confusion now obtaining in Europe.   That is what comes of trying to act the error that the life of nations is based on force.   But when truth is put upon the stage you will observe the opposite—and you may see it in your own life as well as in the history of the world.   The action, which may begin confusedly and with many obstructions, will advance step by step towards harmony and order and significance.   It yields convincing results, while the other thing becomes more meaningless the further it proceeds.   It shines more and more to the perfect day, while the other thing darkens and darkens until at last it falls to pieces and becomes a "tale told by an idiot."   Acted error is always like that.

If, then, it be true that the highest cannot be spoken, what follows?   It follows that we must not look for the highest in the world of human speech. Speech can tell us high things, and it can tell them with great beauty and force, but the highest requires another medium of expression. Let us beware of the eloquence of mere speech, and ground nothing upon it which cannot be confirmed by the higher eloquence of action. Truths which have nothing but speech to recommend them are apt to degenerate into cant. Truths which are eloquently argued for but not acted—such truths I find very hard *We need truths acted.* to distinguish from lies. You may prove them up to the hilt, but until you act them they will convince nobody.

Mr. Lloyd George, in the address he gave not long ago as Rector of Edinburgh University, told his audience that government nowadays is government by talk. I am afraid it is only too true. And what may we conclude from that? We may conclude that any community that is governed by talk is not governed by the highest. For the highest cannot be spoken. We may also conclude that it is not grounded on reality. For reality and the highest are one and the same. Neither can be fully spoken.

Both can be acted. In acting the one we act the other.

As an illustration of all this, take the general question, so prominent in earnest minds, of finding remedies for the great evils which afflict our civilisation. In our present methods of dealing with that type of problem we show a great want of the sense of reality. The real remedies for these things are those that can be acted with the utmost promptitude. They lose their reality when we allow them to become involved in the delays of endless discussion. The cry of human need is very urgent. It is a cry for help *here and now* like that of a drowning man; not a cry for help at some indefinite period in the future. But if our remedy is one which cannot be applied until we have talked ourselves out, then we shall have to reckon with all the suffering, the miseries, the shipwrecks and calamities that have to be endured *in the meantime,* and the tale of all that will rise up in judgment against us. If we had the sense of reality the thought of what is going on in the meantime would weigh upon us like a nightmare. Government by talk! Well, of course there is something to be said for it.

But is it not a tragical thing when we become
so absorbed in the talking, and in listening to it,
that our ears grow deaf to the cry of human
need, to the cry of the millions who perish in
the meantime? The essence of reality in these
things is acted promptitude.

Ladies and gentlemen, I often think that we
are losing the faculty of acted promptitude.
We may listen too long to pulpit arguments and
to parliamentary eloquence. There is a saying
of Christ's which comes vividly to my mind in
this connection. "Agree with thine adversary
quickly," He says, "whilst thou art in the way
with him." *"Quickly."* Make the terms of
your agreement short, clear, prompt and decisive. Settle with thine adversary *on the spot*.
Do not embark on an endless discussion! Do
not leave the amount of reparation you expect
him to pay an unknown quantity! Do not prolong the period of payment over thirty or forty
years! *Get it over and done with whilst thou
are in the way with him.* I see statesmanship
in that. I feel the reality of it. I hear the
voice of a leadership which the world has lost.

Or take another example: a larger specimen

of the same thing. It refers to the League of Nations.

If we consider the League of Nations in a purely abstract, logical or academical way we might easily persuade ourselves that no such thing could ever come into existence. How, we may ask, can the nations ever form a league unless they are already in league to form it? We seem to be in a vicious circle. That is how the matter presents itself when considered in a purely abstract, logical or academic way.

But human history does not move by the rules of this logic. What logic proves to be impossible is sometimes rendered easy by the march of events. This actually happened five years ago.

When the statesmen of the world met in Paris to make the peace they were to all intents and purposes a League of Nations. The Covenant, the wording of it, had still to come, but the fact of it, the reality of it, the League that was to form the League, was already there in germ. It was there in the persons of the statesmen assembled—if they had only known it. They had a common object—that of making a lasting peace, the very thing a League of Nations has to do; and they had a common chance of making it such as the world has never had before nor since. History had beaten logic; the march of events had broken the vicious circle.

Had this group of statesmen, not yet bearing the name of a league, but having the reality within its grasp, proceeded forthwith to *act* the League all would have been well. But they did something else. They *worded* the League, and in the rest of their Treaty they *acted* something that was not the League. They worded the right thing and they acted the wrong; and overlooking the significance of what they were acting, they fondly hoped, as all of us in these days are apt to do, that the thing they were *wording* would do the business. The old order was restored to the acting stage of history; the thing that human need was crying for was flung back into the region of discussion. Future ages will look back on all that as a very tragical moment in the history of mankind.

In all this I am trying to answer that most difficult of questions—What do we mean by reality? I am suggesting that reality is to be found in those highest truths which cannot be spoken, but can be, and are, embodied in deeds. Let us follow that out a little further.

Truth, Beauty and Goodness, we have often been told, are the ultimate realities of the universe. And so I believe they are. But what should we know of Truth if we merely heard men speaking truthfully, and never saw them acting truthfully? What should we know of Beauty if it came to us only by hearsay, if there were no artists to create it and we had never tried to make a thing beautiful ourselves? What should we know of Goodness if we had only heard it talked about and never seen a good man or a noble woman? Act truthfully, make things beautiful, live well—there are no other means by which any of us, even though he should happen to have the largest brain on earth, will ever find out what Truth, Beauty and Goodness really are. No amount of hearsay will reveal them to us. No speech-making, however eloquent, will bring us one hair's breadth nearer to them. I do not say there is no use in talking about these things—for am I not talking about them myself at this moment? —but the talk has no meaning, no power, no life, until the thing is *done*.

Or take another word which some regard as indicating the highest reality in the universe —the word Duty. What is Duty? I answer that the wisest man among us will never understand what Duty is until he *does* it. You may know all the philosophers have written on that subject—and they have written a great deal— and, on the strength of what you have learnt in that way you may graduate with the highest honours in man's University, but in God's University you will be treated as a total ignoramus and never get a single mark *until your duty is done*. "Do the duty that lies nearest—and thy next duty shall become clear to thee"; and finally the divine nature of all duty shall shine before thee in its splendour as an acted reality. Duty by hearsay, duty by argument, duty by eloquence, duty by propaganda—before God, there is not much in all that! Whether "government by talk" is a real thing or not I leave you to decide; but duty by talk is mere "wind and empty babble." If you want an example of those highest things which cannot be spoken but can be acted you have it in duty. Act it first and then the words you use about it will have mean-

Duty

*one learns
by doing
it.*

ing. Leave it unacted and the words will avail nothing.

Nay, worse than that. When the highest things have been turned into themes of eloquence, or into subjects for the war of minds between contentious philosophers, and when everybody is eager to talk about them, there is a terrible danger that the habit of arguing about these things, and talking eloquently and learnedly about them, may become a substitute for doing them. Oh, that danger is terrible indeed, greater than most of us are aware of, and it is one to which we easily succumb without knowing what has happened to us—the danger of letting the mere discussion of the highest become a substitute for the reality of it as acted on the stage of life! I rather think that some of the deepest troubles of our civilisation may be set down to that. The schools are suffering from it; the universities are suffering from it; the Churches are suffering from it; the Government is suffering from it.

Thomas Carlyle said these things three-quarters of a century ago, and if you haven't listened to him I can hardly hope you will listen to me. He warned us of the dangers of speech-

making, and urged us to cultivate a meditative
silence. On that road, he said, men and nations are going straight to the bottomless pit.
To speech as the *preliminary* to action he gave
all honour—but what he saw in the world about
him was speech made into the *substitute* for action—discussion and speech-making run to such
a head that men were losing sight of the prime
necessity to act the things they were talking
about. The very facility they had acquired for
talking about their duty was blinding them to
the fact that they were not doing it. There is
a piercing truth in that! He saw another
thing. If you want your speech about the
highest things *to keep true* you must *continually*
act the thing you are speaking about. If you do
it only by fits and starts, and fill up the in-
tervals with talking about it and arguing for it,
your speech will degenerate into lying and into
cant. And then he warned us—in words which
I am afraid have been forgotten but ought to
be remembered—that if that kind of thing went
on much longer some terrible catastrophe would
overtake us. "It will appear sufficiently tragical," he said, "long after I am away out of it."
When I think of the Great War, of the causes

of it, which largely consisted in cant and lying, and of the consequences of it as we may now see them in Europe, I often ask myself whether Carlyle's prophecy is not already come true.

So I return to my plea that we should look for reality in the field of action, that we should school ourselves to think of the highest as that which can be acted and not as that which can be spoken only. Speak it we cannot. Act it we can, thereby making it clear to ourselves and communicating it clearly to others.

That principle—which I shall apply in a moment both to religion and to education—seems to me confirmed by what I can observe of this amazing universe in which I find myself. The deepest truths of the universe are acted rather than spoken. What most impresses me is the deep *silence* of the universe, coupled with its unimaginable activity. I was recently hearing a distinguished man of science describing the wonders in the nebula of Andromeda—that faint mist of light in the depths of the firmament which the naked eye can sometimes detect —magnitudes so vast, forces so stupendous, operations so immense, and yet so minute, that thought simply staggers in the presence of them. What a nebula! the particles of it, the apparent dust of it, composed of enormous bodies, many times the diameter of the sun, burning with inconceivable heat and swinging in beautiful orbits with inconceivable velocity? What can we make of that? The facts of astronomy are so overwhelming, so stupefying, that there are moments when human speech is stricken dumb, and one is almost tempted to cry like a child in the dark or even to howl like a dog, which is the dog's way, I suppose, of expressing his cosmic emotion. Verily, the highest cannot be spoken: the mere vastness of it completely baffles us. "The stars above us and the graves beneath us." Great God, what a universe! And yet we discuss it over our teacups as though it were a thing we carried in our waistcoat pockets.

As I listened to that astronomer a question forced itself upon me which you too must often have asked when looking at the starry firmament above and at the moral law within—the two things, you will remember, which Kant says struck him dumb. "Is all that," I asked myself, "alive or dead?" The moral law within, that I know is alive, more intensely alive than

anything else that I know of. But is its life a
mere accident, a trivial by-product of the universal industries, while all the rest is stone
dead? Or is it part of a larger and longer life,
which embraces the starry firmament above and
links me in a spiritual unity with these amazing
activities in the nebula of Andromeda? Of two
things, one. Either the whole is alive together,
moral law and starry firmament dancing to the
same immortal melody, or else the life that I
have, moral law and all, is not worth very much.
For myself I cannot but believe that it is all
alive, not as a vegetable is alive, but as I am
alive myself. I think there is a *soul* in it just
as there is a soul in me. I cannot think of all
that as dead—while you and I and the rest of
us on this insignificant planet are alive as soli-
tary exceptions. All which has been far better
said than I can ever say it in Addison's beautiful hymn, the presence of which in our hymn
books compensates for much of the nonsense
you will often find alongside of it.

> "What though in solemn silence all
> Move round the dark terrestrial ball;
> What though no real voice nor sound
> Amid their radiant orbs be found;

In reason's ear they all rejoice
And utter forth a glorious voice,
For ever singing as they shine,
The hand that made us is divine."

In the last analysis there are only two possible doctrines, or philosophies, as to the nature
of this mighty universe. The one holds it to be
alive, and the other holds it to be dead. And
now, judging not by the beliefs that men pro-
fess, but by the beliefs that they act, the only
true criterion, which of these two philosophies
is the actual creed of our civilisation?

From all I can observe of the practice of our
civilisation, both on the large scale of its public
policies and on the small scale of the private
valuations which individuals place on the goods
of life, it seems to me pretty plain that men,
unconsciously for the most part, are holding the
belief that the universe is *dead*. They are treating the world as a dead and passive thing that
is there for them to make use of and to exploit,
to turn into marketable commodities and
money's worth. And if that is how they treat
the whole world, is it to be wondered at that
sometimes they treat one another in much the
same way? A vast machine whose forces can

be harnessed to their own aims, but which itself feels nothing, knows nothing, cares nothing and resents nothing of what men do with it. The practice of our civilisation suggests that men, generally, have taken it for granted that they are living in that kind of a world. And a great deal of current teaching says explicitly that it is so; though now and then you hear a voice that says that it is *not* so.

What would we expect to become of a civilisation based upon the assumption that the universe is *dead,* if the actual fact should turn out to be that the universe is *alive,* fully aware of the tricks men are playing with it and quite capable of resenting them? What if the universe, being alive, is not asking us to exploit it but to love it and to enjoy it? There will be trouble for that civilisation. Such a universe, we may be sure, will not altogether approve of our present methods of exploitation and will sooner or later give us a reminder of its disapproval.

I have read somewhere an Eastern story of a great monarch who, having conquered half the earth, resolved to build himself a marvellous palace to commemorate his victories. He laid the foundations on a wide platform of rock and dug out the side of a mountain for the stones and felled the forests for his timbers. One day, when all was complete, and a great revel was going on inside, the King discovered to his astonishment that he and his palace were sailing in mid air. What he had taken for a platform of rock was the smooth back of a mighty monster which had been asleep for ten thousand years; the mountain was a wart on its head, and the great forests were its outstretched wings. The noise of his revelries had awakened it and now it was flying away with him. Presently the monster gave itself a mighty shake, and the King and his palace were flung headlong into the sea.

Some have thought that the Great War was due to similar causes. Civilisation got a shake and a good many high-reared structures toppled over. Perhaps it was the living universe showing its resentment at being treated as though it were dead.

This theory of a dead universe, which makes it out to be a machine, can be impressively defended on the field of argument. Many minds, not of the meanest capacity, have accepted it because the argument led them that way. But the final test of its reality will be on the field of action. What account does the theory of a dead universe give of itself when dramatised in the policies of nations and put upon the stage of social life, as it has been now in the history of Europe ever since the birth of mechanical science three hundred years ago? How does it *act?*

Judging by the results of the experiment up to date, I am inclined to answer that the theory of a dead universe breaks down. It resembles a badly written drama which cannot be acted. After acting rather showily for a time, and giving promise of great things, the drama reaches a stage when it no longer moves to a clear issue, but begins to degenerate into meaningless confusion. The actors lose their co-operative purpose and, instead of playing their parts in harmony, fall upon one another, and fill the stage with anarchy and riot, such as you see in Europe to-day. When I think of all that has happened during the last nine years, and is happening now, the conviction forces itself upon me that this attempt to treat the universe as a dead thing for man to exploit and make use of can never be made into the basis of the human drama. No lasting civilisation can be built upon it. There is nothing but confusion at the end of it—such confusion as we see all around us at this moment. The play won't act. The plot doesn't work out.

Many great minds both in ancient and modern times have believed that the universe is alive. Among the ancients Plato, the Stoics, the author of the Book of Job; among the moderns, Immanuel Kant, and the great idealists, Goethe, Wordsworth, Shelley, William Blake, Tennyson, Ruskin, Carlyle—to name only a few. They have held the universe to be alive as a man is alive, with intelligence and with purpose, with justice and with love. Every one of them has foreseen that a civilisation or a society which treats the universe as dead cannot maintain itself for long, but is bound to go down sooner or later under the impact of the eternal laws it is unconsciously violating.

This theory of the living universe—I would rather call it a vision than a theory—is the summary of all those highest truths that cannot be spoken, except by way of hints and distant allusions. That is not mysticism, but the one practical philosophy.

Every man's life is an acted philosophy of one kind or another—and, as I said a moment ago, there are in the last analysis only two possible philosophies. The acting of a living universe is what we call the Kingdom of God, which is not meat and drink, but righteousness, joy and peace, the only form of human life in harmony with a universe that is alive. Hear the words of one of the greatest of biologists, Dr. J. S. Haldane of Oxford—for the men of science are not all on the side of a dead universe, by no means! "The material world"—think of the nebula in Andromeda—"the material world," he says, "which has been taken for a world of blind mechanism is in reality the spiritual world seen very partially. . . . The only real world is the spiritual world." But if you would find its reality do not content yourself with *saying* it is spiritual, but *act* it and reproduce it and make it a living thing. The humblest bit of matter, half real as it is, has more claim on our reverence than the most eloquent unreality that ever got itself decked out in human speech.

Christianity is richer than any other religion

I know of in actable truth. I say they *can* be acted; I do not say they always *are*. None of them are easy to act. But we must carefully distinguish between those that are hard to act and those that cannot be acted at all, but only talked about and argued for. There are some of these latter, and they mark the weak spots. One of the tasks awaiting Christian theologians to-day is to sift out those parts of Christianity which cannot be acted and to stand firm on those which can.

God, Freedom, and Immortality, the main pillars of every religion, are all actable: God, by living a god-like life—the only way in which you can finally convince yourself or anybody else that God exists; Freedom by silent and heroic service; Immortality by asserting your citizenship in heaven and claiming your membership in the Communion of Saints. There are others: think of them for yourselves.

And what of the education we are giving to children in the schools and to young men and women in the universities? Is it actable education? Is it of the kind they can follow up and develop into the continuous culture of a life-time? Will it help them to enjoy the universe and to love it, or will it merely swell the army of exploiters who would make what they can out of the blind machine, and so increase the confusion into which that unhappy drama is now drifting? Will their education cease the moment they leave school, as a thing for which they have no further use, or will it continue and prolong itself to the end of their days as a vital motive for good work? According as the answer falls out one way or another, you have the difference between an education which is a reality and an education which is a sham. Education will become *real* when all the children and all the adults are being trained to play their parts as living members of a living universe. Here, again, the task of educationists is to sift out the shams, of which there are many, from the realities.

And, in general, the thing that we are preaching in our pulpits and teaching in our schools and universities, is it only something we argue for and grow contentious over and work up into eloquence? Then away with it, for it is mere cant! Or is it a plan of action, a scheme of noble living, a thing we are doing and mean to do? Then stick to it, for it is a reality!

I will end by giving an actual instance of what I mean by reality in education.

Not long ago I met one of our great school-masters—a veteran in that high service. "Where in your time-table do you teach religion?" I asked him. "We teach it all day long," he answered. "We teach it in arithmetic, by accuracy. We teach it in language, by learning to say, what we mean—'yea, yea and nay, nay.' We teach it in history, by humanity. We teach it in geography, by breadth of mind. We teach it in handicraft, by thoroughness. We teach it in astronomy, by reverence. We teach it in the playground, by fair play. We teach it by kindness to animals, by courtesy to servants, by good manners to one another, and by truthfulness in all things. We teach it by showing the children that we, their elders, are their friends and not their enemies." "But what," I said, "about the different denominations? Have you no trouble with the parents?" "None at all," he replied; "we have half a dozen denominations. But we treat the children, not as members of this Church or that, but as members of the school, and we show them that, as members of the school, in work and in play, they are members of one another. We teach them to build the Church of Christ out of the actual relations in which they stand to their teachers and their schoolfellows, because we believe that unless they learn to build it where they are they will not learn to build it afterwards anywhere else." "Do you talk much to them about religion?" I then asked. "Not much," he said, "just enough to bring the whole thing to a point now and then." Finally he added a remark that struck me—"I do not want religion," he said, "brought into this school from outside. *What we have of it we grow ourselves.*"

There, ladies and gentlemen, you have reality *both* in religion and in education.

And now to sum up.

We are all tired of shams—shams in religion, in education, in politics. We want reality. I suggest to you that reality is an actable thing rather than a speakable thing. Seek for reality in what you mean to do, not in what you are fond of saying. Treat Christianity as an actable religion, and distrust all forms of it which consist in merely saying this or saying that. Think of the universe about you as alive with a spirit that for ever acts the truths on which the universe reposes. Give to the children an education which shall lead up stage by stage to the acting of Truth, the acting of Beauty, the acting of Goodness.

II: CIVILISATION IN A LIVING UNIVERSE

II: Civilisation in a Living Universe

In the last lecture I said that the cry of human need, as it goes up from our great populations, is very urgent and peremptory. On the other hand, the machinery we have for coping with these needs is dilatory, and, because dilatory, often ineffective. An enormous amount of human wreckage takes place in the meantime, while democracies are making up their minds and while Governments are "exchanging notes." At this moment [1] human wreckage is going on all over central Europe. It is one of the drawbacks of "government by talk," that the bitter cry of these perishing multitudes gets drowned in the voice of mere debate. In striving with one another for dialectical mastery we forget that those whom we would help are passing beyond the reach of our remedies. The dying patient is lost sight of in the disputes of the

[1] April 1923.

consulting physicians. These interim sufferings of mankind are a heavy indictment of our present methods. They cast a doubt on the value of our political civilisation.

Take the question of armaments as an example. Of late years there has been an immense discussion of this matter; it has been the subject of many conferences, of hundreds of political meetings, and a vast amount of propaganda. What is the result? While we have been talking about the reduction of armaments, the standing armies of Europe have increased by nearly twenty per cent. In 1913 they numbered 3,700,000. To-day they number 4,300,000. In spite of the fact that the great armies of Germany and Austria have been almost wiped out, there are in Europe to-day 600,000 more men under arms than there were in 1913. The Eighth Article of the Covenant of the League of Nations runs as follows: "The members of the League recognise that the maintenance of peace requires the reduction of national armaments to the lowest point consistent with national safety." And yet Sir Frederick Maurice assures us that some of the new States created by the Peace Treaty are at this moment groaning under military burdens heavier than they had to bear when they were parts of the great military empires. Government by talk has not effected very much in that direction. The reduction of armaments is a far more formidable problem to-day than it was ten years ago. Sir Henry Wilson, in the last speech he made before he was assassinated, described the situation as simply "terrifying."

One of the most striking features of our time is the enormous amount of earnest propaganda that is going on in behalf of good causes. Viewed by itself, it is an encouraging phenomenon, because it shows that, after all, mankind means well. But a certain disquietude arises when we compare it with the actual results to which it leads. Many of the social evils we are attacking resemble the evil of armaments in rapidly growing from bad to worse while we are making up our minds what to do with them. They do not stand still while we are composing our perorations. With some of them it is literally a question of "now or never." They are like those cases in surgery when the surgeon tells us that unless he operates immediately the patient will die. They call for prompt and decisive action.

But democratic Governments are seldom allowed by the public behind them to "operate immediately," even when the matter is urgent and it is a question of life and death—in which respect they are perhaps at a disadvantage with Governments of another kind. A long process of discussion has to be gone through, a campaign of propaganda has to be conducted, before operation is decided on. By that time it is frequently too late. Sad tales of lost opportunities present themselves, of which perhaps the tale of Ireland is the saddest. Indeed I am afraid it must be said that much of our public life resolves itself into an attempt to make good by propaganda what has been lost by procrastination. It measures the extent of our lost opportunities. And the danger is that we fall into the speech-making habit, and lose at the same time the faculty of promptitude, the dust of controversy blinding us to the opportunities that are slipping by, perhaps never to return, so that we may say, with Hamlet, that "enterprises of great pith and moment, with this regard their currents turn awry, and lose the name of action."

The League of Nations is one of them. The evils it seeks to cure will not bear indefinite postponement; they, obviously, are of the kind that rapidly go from bad to worse. The patient is desperately sick. We must not yield to our bad habit of procrastinating in the hope that further discussion will make all good. To-morrow the crisis may have passed beyond the reach of our remedies. While we are debating how the nations may be prevented from hurting one another, they *are* hurting one another. These things don't stand still. Discussion of them is, of course, necessary; but not *endless* discussion. There had been plenty of it four years ago; but we seem no nearer the moment of decisive action now than we were then.

I have been told that it will take the League twenty years to acquire the authority it needs. Twenty years! Here is a case where "immediate operation" is necessary and you tell me it will be twenty years before the instruments are ready. There is something wrong about all this.

If the League of Nations ever becomes a

reality, I apprehend that it will have to be a body capable of swift decisions, of great promptitude. Most of the problems presented to it will be of the "now or never" kind. The League must not linger over its problems, as the British Parliament lingered for a century over the problem of Ireland. That will never do when great catastrophes are imminent. There will not be time for many speeches, and those for which there is time must be to the point. There will be work in the League for silent and heroic men, even if they are not wanted anywhere else. "Government by talk" may be all very well in its proper place, though, for my part, I don't know where the proper place is to be found. But in the League of Nations it would be disastrous.

There is grave reason for doubting whether statesmen and politicians who have become saturated with the habits of our talking civilisation are quite the best men for the swift and urgent business the League will have to transact. In that enterprise there must be no waiting to see which way the cat jumps, or what happens to their pilot balloons, or what sort of a Press they get next morning, or what their constituents will think of it. I imagine we shall have to find a different kind of man for that work.

It may be asserted, as a proposition admitting of no dispute, that the success of a League of Nations depends, ultimately, on the quality of the men who conduct its business. Their moral qualifications must be exceptionally high. Even allowing, what I am not sure of, that the brilliant parliamentary orator, the astute manager of parties, the effective leader at a general election, is the best kind of man for domestic politics, it does not follow that he would be the best kind of man for entrusting with the business of a League of Nations. Possibly he might be the worst. I am inclined to think that he would be.

Our League of Nations man must be a man capable of working for distant aims, and with time given him for achieving them. He must be one whom we can trust with a long dated commission. We must not say to him, as democracy says to its political operators, "You are liable to be turned out at a moment's notice." We must say to him, as we say to our judges, "This is your life's work, and, before God, you must stick to it till it is finished." Short of the man whom we can trust to that extent we have not found the man we want. Before all else he must be a Trustee. The qualities we reverence in a Trustee rather than those we admire in a politician are the qualities needed for the League of Nations.

It follows that our League of Nations man, like our judges, should have nothing to do with electioneering. He should be free to devote himself to the primary interests of justice and fair dealing, undisturbed by the secondary interests that gather round elections and by the dodgery and artifice that go with that business. Plato said that the world would never be well governed till philosophers became kings; and politicians, when they hear the saying quoted, are wont to smile. But there must be no smiling when the League of Nations is in question. If the men who are to conduct that enterprise are not philosophers they must at all events be more than politicians. They must be Trustees. And that in a double sense. First in the sense that they are worthy of trust, and, then, in the sense that those who appoint them do, actually, trust them.

Are such men to be found in these days? I believe they are, and that in abundance. Some of them go into politics, and find, when they get there, that the double part of trustee and politician is not easy to play. But most of them never go into politics at all. At this moment the men most needed for a League of Nations, most capable of grasping its issues and conducting its business, are outside of politics. If challenged I could name offhand a dozen men in Europe who would do this business better than any dozen you could pick out from the Chancelleries and the Foreign Offices and the Cabinets, from the parties in power or from the parties in opposition. There we touch the weakest spot in our political civilisation, the weakness which all the devices of democracy and all the extensions of the franchise have so far not succeeded in overcoming. *It fails to employ its best men for its highest work.*

But we are getting into deep and dangerous waters. Several times I have alluded to our "political civilisation," and you will be asking me what I mean by that. Deep and dangerous as the waters are, let us plunge into them at once. They lie between us and the shore we have to reach. I am now come to the most difficult part of my lecture.

When we hear of "civilisation" we are apt to think that only one kind is possible—that, namely, with which we ourselves are familiar. We think of our democratic Government, of our representative system, our methods of doing justice and keeping order, our great industries, our mechanical and scientific inventions, and all that we name "civilisation." That is what suits *us,* and we are apt to think that it suits *everybody.* As a matter of fact there are millions of men, of enlightened men, living in the world to-day, mostly in the East, who have been born and bred under a different type of civilisation altogether and who, when they come into contact with ours, do not admire it and do not want it. Sir Henry Maine, in his great work on Popular Government, reminds us that our type, which we think the only one possible, is thoroughly detested by the great majority of the human race. And I observe that Professor Radhakrishnan, of the University of Calcutta, says the same thing. "There are men in the East," he says in a recent article, "who if they have eyes left to weep with, spend sleepless nights in cursing God because he has allowed these civilisers to get into their lands." Well, such cursers of God may be wrong. But the words remind us that ours is not the only type of civilisation men want and care for. There is another, which has flourished in the past, and which still exists in Eastern countries, though it has been greatly changed by contact with ours.

Our civilisation is a peculiar thing. The general form of it, indeed, is ancient, but the special form we are familiar with dates from the development of combative nationalism, and is hardly more than three hundred years old. Another kind existed in Europe alongside of it, under the protection of the Church, for many centuries before these developments took place, and there are specimens of it in the Eastern parts of the world, though threatened and decaying. Our civilisation is, on the whole, of the conquering type; but the other is not out for conquest, and has never developed its conquering aptitudes, so that naturally it stands a poor chance against ours.

The two types of civilisation in question are

the *political* and the *cultural*. Ours is the political type, which for the last three hundred years has been gradually winning and beating the other off the field. The question is, Will it hold its victory for ever? Will political civilisation as we know it conquer the whole world and become established as the final order of mankind? Or may it be that mankind, after developing political civilisation to its uttermost, and spreading it everywhere, and getting out of it all that it is capable of yielding, will discover that it is not so completely satisfactory as it was thought to be, and begin to look with wistful eyes to cultural civilisation, so long discarded, as on the whole a better thing? Before answering that question let us try to get a clear idea of the two types.

The main feature of political civilisation is the *struggle for power,* between nation and nation, or between class and class. That struggle takes two forms. First, there is the struggle to *gain* power while nations or classes are extending their conquests; and then the struggle to *keep* the power which has been won, and save it from being encroached upon by the others, who have done the same thing. At this second

stage of the struggle we get what is called the
"balance of power," the most unstable kind of
balance under the sun. When nations go to war
in these days they generally give it out that
they are not bent upon conquest, but are only
defending the conquests and the power they
have won already—which is sometimes true
and sometimes false. Their object is, they say,
to prevent the balance of power from being upset. But this balance of power is a very precari-
ous thing. Even if you make the balance perfect by treaties or diplomatic arrangements,
it may be upset at any moment by a sudden increase of wealth or of scientific invention or by
the growth of population in any one of the
nations concerned, and by many other things
which no statesmanship can control. Terrible
wars may break out even in a time when no
nation is definitely out for conquest. The question of *keeping* the power they have already
won, always changing its balance from inside
causes, is quite enough to start the fighting.
No statesman, however far-seeing and humane,
can really control the balance of power, though
we are always expecting our Foreign Minis-
ters to control it. In a world where scientific

invention and economic progress and the growth of population go on at different rates in different countries, the balance is always tending to upset itself. It is, as I said, the most unstable balance under the sun.

Now look at the civilisation of culture. And before I go on let me say that the word culture, as I am using it, does not mean superficial varnish either of one kind or another. By culture I mean the process by which the powers and faculties of human beings are liberated, organised, educated and developed. The main object in the civilisation of culture is not to increase the power of the State but to promote the best mode of living among the citizens, and it attaches more importance to their personal characters than it does to their possessions. It aims first at human development. You get an idea of it in Aristotle's definition of the State. The State, he says, is a means to the good life. Of how many States now existing in the world can we say that they go whole-heartedly for helping their citizens to live the good life? Yet that is what cultural civilisation aims at doing.

There are two causes which make it extremely difficult for us to form a clear notion of a civilisation of culture. First, we are so accustomed to the political sort, with its basis in the struggle for power, our minds are so saturated with habits of thought that have sprung from it, that we can hardly imagine any other kind existing, and so take the other kind for mere moonshine when we hear it talked about. The second reason is that pure examples of cultural civilisation are hardly to be found in the modern world. The examples that exist are mostly mere remnants, and they become more and more adulterated by contact with the political variety. They are not good examples, and the consequence is that, in order to understand what cultural civilisation is capable of, we have to use our imaginations, which many of us are not very willing to do. I ask you to note the point that cultural civilisation is relatively free from the struggle for power. I don't say that the struggle for power has no place in it at all, but it is always a secondary thing, and not the primary thing it is apt to become with civilisation of the political kind.

Now let us ask, why is it that, in spite of the belief that most of us have in the reasonableness and the necessity of a League of Nations, and

in spite of the fact that so many leading statesmen in all countries may be said to have pledged
themselves to it, we find nevertheless that the
League of Nations is extraordinarily difficult
to set on foot as a working arrangement?

The reasons lie in the political nature of the
civilisation we are dealing with. It is well-nigh
impossible to devise any form for such a League
which does not demand from the nations concerned in it, and especially from the great nations, something which they are very unwilling
to give up. It demands a considerable surrender of their power, or, as we call it, their sov-
ereign rights, for the common good. In asking
these power-loving nations to give up some portion of the power they have so long fought for,
and shed so much precious blood to win, we
are asking them, as it were, to give up their very
nature, almost their very souls. And that is
more than they can do. There is no Government in Europe or America at the present day
which would not be instantly wrecked by the
political forces behind it if it were to surrender
any considerable portion of its territory, its
wealth or its power. No party Government dare
do such a thing. The more you look into that,

the more clearly you see how immensely difficult it must always be to make a League of Nations out of a political civilisation. We are often told that a change of heart would do the business. Precisely: but that does not help us unless we know what form the change of heart is to take and how it is to be brought about. Here *saying* that a change of heart is necessary will not accomplish much.

But now imagine—and I grant you it is not easy—that we had a civilisation organised on the basis of culture. Imagine the world divided into a number of States each of which had chosen, for its main object, to help its citizens to "live the good life," to liberate their faculties, to develop their powers of intelligence and enjoyment to the utmost possible pitch—the sort of State that Aristotle had in mind. How comparatively easy the formation of a real community of nations would now become! I will not say there would be no difficulties, but the chief difficulties that now beset us would vanish. Where now we have points of repulsion we should then have points of attraction. Any State or Nation that was in earnest in helping its citizens to live the good life would then perceive that it needed the co-operation of all the other States that were out for the same thing. Culture in the sense in which I am using the word, not as mere varnish, but as human development, is essentially an international and co-operative enterprise. We haven't to *make* it so by compacts and treaties and covenants; it *is* so by its own nature. Make culture, in that large sense, your basis and a League of Nations would almost come of itself.

An impossible dream, you will tell me. Well, perhaps. But there are certain things now going on in the world which incline me to think that "impossible" is rather too strong a word to put upon it. I don't like that word "impossible" when the destinies of mankind are in question. Man is a creative being—that is, a conqueror of the impossible.

Keep a close watch, for example, on the movement for education. Look at it steadily, and ask what it all means. You will observe that in all countries, more perhaps abroad than at home, the demand is slowly gathering force, not only for more education, but for a better kind. While other movements go up and down, you will see this movement continually going up. What do you make of that? What interpretation do you put upon it? Does it only mean that people generally are growing keen for a little varnish? That I should set down as a very shallow interpretation. There is something deeper and greater. The true meaning is that men and women everywhere are becoming conscious in themselves of powers and of faculties to which our political civilisation has never given a proper chance. They are crying out for the liberation of those powers, for the development of those faculties. They are demanding the civilisation of culture. They are asking the State to help them to live the good life. They may not use these words, but that is the thing, the reality they are after. There is a shifting of the basis of civilisation in the direction of culture. Watch that movement for education and you will see that every step it takes forward is a step towards the point where the nations will find a common object, and become a co-operative community.

The conclusion I suggest is this: that a community of nations will always remain an extremely difficult thing to bring about in a civilisation based on power. But it would become comparatively easy in one based on culture. Further we see in education a possible force, which may, in course of time, if it is allowed to develop, change the one thing into the other. May not this be the very "change of heart" we are looking for: a growing desire for cultural civilisation; a change in our habits of valuation: the spiritual interests which go with culture being rated higher than the material interests that go with power? Whenever we meet a man who realises the value of education, may we not say that the needed change of heart has begun in that man?

I should like, if you will have patience, to draw the contrast between the two kinds of civilisation a little more sharply.

The civilisation of power aims at the *exploitation of the world,* which is thought of as a dead or mechanical thing, existing that men may exploit it. That of culture aims at the *development of man,* thought of as the citizen of a living universe which can be loved, enjoyed and reverenced; education being the name of the process which leads him to love, enjoy and reverence it. That is one contrast—political civilisation for a dead universe, cultural civilisation for a live one.

Again, in the civilisation of power, "government" bulks bigger than anything else in the mind of the citizen, political reform is the accepted means of social salvation, and the statesman is the most important personage. Man is thought of as a being whose first need is to be well *governed*. In the cultural kind, on the other hand, man is thought of as a being whose first need is to be well *taught*. Teach him well and you won't have much trouble in governing him. Accordingly the most important personage now is, not the statesman, but the teacher, and education ranks higher than politics. It did so in the ideal State outlined by Plato in his *Laws,* where the Minister of Education is the Prime Minister.

The contrast may be further sharpened. Why is government so immensely important in societies such as ours? The reason is that the main energies of those societies are devoted to the pursuit of material wealth, to the creation of material values. Now the pursuit of wealth is, by its nature, a quarrelsome occupation. It easily becomes provocative and even cruel. If left to take its own course the strong would trample on the weak and the successful would rob one another. Constant legislation is therefore needed to restrain injustice and to keep order among the competing elements; and when nations attain to great riches and to high complexity the amount of legislation needed to maintain their social equilibrium is enormous. Such societies cannot get on without the police, and the law courts behind the police, and an elaborate legislative machinery behind the law courts—all the apparatus of political civilisation.

But in societies that aim at culture—always in the sense I have given to the word—the causes of quarrel become very much less, and if only the culture aimed at be high enough they disappear altogether. The pursuit of human development maintains its own equilibrium. In the kingdom of heaven there are no policemen —at least I have never heard of there being any —and not many lawyers. We can pursue knowledge, or cultivate the fine arts, or practise religion without much danger that the strong will trample on the weak or the successful rob one another. The tendency is rather the other way. Great minds, who are the agents of culture, do not try to keep the little minds down; they try to lift them up to their own level. They are not like the tyrants of the political world. If we heard that a great mind was about to appear we should not think it necessary to tell the police to keep an eye on him, lest he should take advantage of us little people and exploit us for his own advantage. We should be quite sure that a really great mind would do his best for all of us, that he would give his best to us instead of stealing from us the little best we already have. Cultural civilisation therefore is able to get on with the minimum of Government control, while political requires the maximum. In the one, the political apparatus is primary; in the other, secondary. The contrast between the two is pretty sharp at that point.

Now let us apply all this to the Community of Nations. If you proceed on a political basis, the problem becomes one of government; you will need all the apparatus of government; and especially you must devise some means of enforcing obedience. How the League is to carry on without a powerful international police baffles my comprehension. If policemen are needed to keep order among unarmed citizens they will be needed still more to keep order among warlike nations, some of them armed to the teeth with the deadliest weapons conceivable. But the creation of an international police is an extraordinarily difficult proposition, the danger being that the national quarrels it is created to suppress may infect the ranks of the police itself, and so shatter its cohesion before it gets to work. And yet, so long as we are working on a basis of power, and with political elements, I do not see how any progress can be made until this question is solved.

Indeed when we come to that point I, for one, should despair of the League were it not for my belief that its chances lie in a different field altogether. As I see the matter, only a cultural civilisation can solve the problem of a community of nations. I am firmly persuaded that one day it will be solved on that field. No doubt it had to begin as a political experiment. But our very failures to carry it out on political ground, which are becoming more apparent every day, will open our eyes to the necessity of solving it on a higher level.

In all this I would not be understood as throwing contempt on political civilisation. It has taught mankind two lessons of supreme value, which could hardly have been learnt in any other way—the lesson of organisation and the lesson of scientific method. What we may hope for in the future is not the loss of these things—that would be a calamity—but their gradual transference from the service of power to the service of culture, from the exploitation of the world to the development of man. In the earth there still exists a vast store of material riches waiting to be appropriated, but the immaterial treasure that lies buried in *man,* waiting for development, is immeasurably greater. All that we have so far done in that domain has merely scratched the surface. What can be achieved when organisation and scientific method, inherited from the struggle for power, have been fully employed in the development of man, we have yet to see.

There have been many cultural civilisations in the world which have gone to wreck through the impact of the political kind that we or our ancestors have created. Are we to conclude on that account that the kind which perished was

inferior to the kind that destroyed it? The
civilisation of ancient Greece was largely cultural, but it went to pieces on contact with the
Roman. Does it follow that the Roman was
the higher of the two? Another example that
I find significant is the Spanish Conquest of
Mexico in the early sixteenth century. In ancient Mexico there was cultural civilisation of a
sort; it was a crude affair, it had some very
ugly features, but with some beautiful ones
alongside of them. It was completely wiped out
by the Spanish conquerors. The Mexicans had
no military organisation to speak of; their government was hardly worth the name; their ar-
mour was made out of the feathers of gorgeous
birds; they had no horses; and their weapons
were such toys as children play with. Naturally they had no chance against the greatest
military power then extant in the world. A
handful of Spanish warriors clothed in mail,
mounted on horses, and furnished with artil-
lery, scattered them like a flock of sheep, hurled
down their temples and burned their cities over
their heads. A similar process has been going
on for more than a century over vast tracts of
Asia, at first to the accompaniment of terrible

bloodshed, and more recently by what is known as peaceful penetration. Japan has deliberately Europeanised herself. The civilisation of China, which most Europeans despise, though few of them understand it, the old Vedic civilisations of India, which we are just beginning to respect, were distinctly cultural. Under contact with the political civilisation of the West they have rocked and tottered and in places have disappeared. Again I ask—Are we to conclude from this that the conquering type is the better? It is an open question; a question which none of us should undertake to answer until he has dismissed prejudice from his mind and thoroughly investigated the facts.

And now let me gather up the threads.

By this time you will perceive that I am asking you to look forward to a time when civilisation will have changed its direction from the quarrelsome work of exploiting the material world to the co-operative work of developing the spirit of man. I ask you to use your imaginations. I ask you to think of the future States of the world as less concerned with the material values of riches and power, and more with the spiritual values that lie hidden, and waiting to be developed, in human nature. Remember Aristotle's definition of the State. Think of a coming time when all the States of the world, or at least the greatest of them, shall have become institutions for helping their citizens to live the good life. That would be cultural civilisation. And don't let yourself be daunted by the word "impossible." Don't say the dream is moonshine until you have carefully examined it.

If now you ask me what is the force, what is the instrument by which so mighty a change will be effected, I answer by pointing to education, including that very highest form of it which we call religion. Religion and education based upon the reality of a living universe, working in partnership, and each gaining enormously in power through its partnership with the other—this is the bridge now in the building, on which mankind will hereafter pass over from the civilisation of power, with its confusions and enmities, to the civilisation of culture with its unity and goodwill. Other bridges there may be also, but this one, I think, will be the main thoroughfare. And again I would say, Do not be disheartened by the fact that the bridge as yet is only in the building, that the piers of it, so to speak, are only just being laid in the deep and dangerous waters. Examine the plan of it, as it exists in the minds of the great architects who are designing it, and you will see that this bridge is meant to carry the weight of a new civilisation.

In the world of education there are some hopeful signs for the believer in cultural civilisation. Great changes have taken place in the last thirty years, and far greater will take place in the next thirty. I will mention three of them; the first referring to children, who are too often overlooked when education is being discussed; the second to the teachers; the third to the system.

First, as to the children. Let me tell you what was said to me the other day by one of the chief actors in London education, a man who has been in the thick of it for forty years. "The most important change in my time," he said, "is this: whereas a generation ago most children hated their school they are now beginning to love it. And they love it not because they are cajoled, or bribed, and things are being made easy for them, but because at last we are treating them with intelligence." And here is a sentence from a letter written to me by the headmistress of a large school in the slums of East London: "Talk about the children creeping unwillingly to school," she writes, "why, we are simply besieged from morning to night." Remember that I am speaking of a change that is only just begun, not of one that is complete. Mark this slowly changing attitude of children toward their education. If their parents do not feel its importance, *they* are beginning to do so. And will not they be the parents of the next generation?

I pass to the teachers. Here a wonderful thing is happening, which does not appear on the surface and which no statistics can reveal, but is to be fond if you look for it—the appearance of genius in the field of education. Genius —what is that? Genius is the great miracle-worker. Genius is the power which does things that ordinary people think impossible. As I go about among teachers I often meet a man or a woman who strikes me as showing the marks of the highest genius. I do not say that all of them are like that; but it is a great thing if only a few of them are, because they tend to raise the rest to their own level. I know of teachers, men and women, who deserve to be ranked, in their own field, with the great geniuses of art, science and religion. Nowhere will you see the creative mind—which is another name for genius—more active to-day than in the field of education. That, too, is a portentous sign.

Last, as to the system. I have spoken before of the division of education into "primary," "secondary" and "higher." Now what I observe to-day is the tendency of *all* education to become *higher* education. I do not mean, of course, that we are teaching in primary schools subjects that ought to be kept for the universities. I mean that the quality is everywhere rising to a higher level, and the geniuses I spoke of a moment ago are pushing it upward to a higher level still. The thing is being better done, and it is being done with a higher object than ever before. Again I am speaking not of changes that are completed but of changes that are beginning.

Note, in the next place, that these changes are going on, not in our own country alone, but in all countries, and in some even more rapidly than here. And then ask yourself this significant question—*Is there no possibility of internationalising all that?* Difficult, I grant you, but not one-half as difficult as the creation of an International Police. What an enormous amount of thought has been spent on devising schemes of international *government*, most of them, alas, unworkable. Suppose that half that amount had been spent, not in repressing what is worst in men, but in drawing out what is best. I venture to say that the Community of Nations would be a much more hopeful prospect than it is. The more I compare the two things, the less I am attracted by this idea of an international policeman and the more am I attracted by the idea of an international teacher. What, for example, forbids us to hope for the rise of an international University? Or an International College for Scientific Research? Why not take advantage of the forces, newly awakened all over the world, which are turning all education into higher education? Those forces are international; they have a natural affinity for one another; they are mutually attractive and mutually helpful; they move towards a common object; they need no compact to balance their claims, and no police to prevent

the strong from trampling on the weak, or the
successful from robbing one another. They
hold the secret of the Community of Nations.
Why not build up from that point?

When all these things are taken into consid-
eration, I submit to you, ladies and gentlemen,
that the idea of education as the bridge between
the old order and the new is not all moonshine,
and that the word "impossible" is far to strong
to be applied to these things.

My last word, which follows from what I
have said, shall be about religion. Is religion
to be a power that unites mankind and makes
for the Community of Nations, or is it to be
what it often has been in the past, a power that
divides?

The history of religion is at times very sad
reading. Its saddest feature is the readiness of
the Churches in all ages to let themselves be
swept into the currents of political civilisation,
adopting its methods and habits of thought, and
often reproducing among themselves that very
struggle for power, that strife as to which shall
be greatest, which they were created to check.
They ought to have kept out of all that. But
they let themselves be swept into it because in

times past "government" seemed the only power with which they could ally themselves. In these days, however, another power has come into being—the power which I have been calling "education." Let them now ally themselves more and more with that. Let them realise the indivisible unity of religion and education. Let them make common cause with the forces that are changing all education into higher education, and so preparing the way for the civilisation of culture, out of which the community of nations will in due time arise. By so doing they will achieve harmony among themselves and they will promote harmony in the great world.

III: IMMORTALITY IN A LIVING UNIVERSE

III: Immortality in a Living Universe

THE observation has often been made that people are least inclined to believe in immortality when others are ostentatiously trying to convince them of it. Discussion of this question is apt to become like a depreciated currency: the more there is of it, the less it is worth. Reasons for denying immortality are abundant, from the more abstruse, in writers like Mr. Bosanquet, who speculates precariously on the nature of "the finite self," to the less abstruse of the Hyde Park orator, who speaks of the "brain" as though he knew all about it and sees no difference between a living body and an animated corpse. The invariable result of presenting the reasons "for" with too much emphasis is that we wake up this host of reasons "against" to answer them; and, in the war of minds which follows, the significance of what we are arguing about is generally lost sight of.

Even the "scientific proof," which spiritualists believe themselves to possess, has had the effect of creating scepticism in many persons whose minds were otherwise at rest upon the subject. For every believer created by those arguments —and no doubt there are many—it would not be hard to find another person who has been inclined the other way. "I had not known sin but for the law," says St. Paul; and there are some who might say with equal truth, "I had not known doubts of my immortality but for your proof that I am immortal." At all events we may be sure that any approach to vociferation in the holder of "proofs," whether of one kind or another, will be swiftly followed by sceptical reactions on the part of those to whom they are addressed. Nor is this a subject for dialectical display.

One of the few predictions that can be made with confidence is that doubt and denial of immortality, as well as belief and affirmation, will always exist. This mixed state of affairs is, perhaps, for the best. I am inclined to think that the value of belief in immortality would diminish if we were all agreed about it, as we are about the multiplication table. And I feel very sure that the value of life for those who deny immortality is raised by the presence in the world of other people who affirm it. This, indeed, is one of the healthiest differences of opinion that exist among mankind. It may be that believers do not get on very well *with* deniers. But *without* the other each side would get on still worse. Nor can I believe that "the great Soul of the world" divides us into sheep and goats according to the side we take on a question so difficult for the wisest to answer.

As a student of philosophy my impression is that this question of immortality forms the background, sometimes unnoticed, often obscured, but always present, to at least three-fourths of the philosophical speculation that has taken place in the world, and to all the great religions. Not enough attention has been given to the part it has played as a motive in prompting speculation, and the subject is waiting for treatment by a thinker who is competent to deal with it. Even philosophers who say nothing about it—and it has become a fashion with many of them to pass it over in silence—owe more to these promptings, both positive and negative, than they seem to be aware of. In the great religions the matter can hardly admit of a doubt, their object being, with the philosophies, either to bring us to a belief in immortality, as in Christianity, or to give us spiritual insight which compensates for the loss of it, as in Buddhism.

Christianity, as presented in the New Testament, stands out with peculiar clearness in this respect. Interpreting the New Testament, not by portions selected to suit our ethical predilections—which has become the modern method of interpretation—but in terms of its unifying motive, there cannot be a doubt that Christianity belongs to the class of religions (there were several of them in antiquity) which aim at conferring immortality, or eternal life, on the believer. The last "enemy" the religion of the New Testament undertakes to destroy is *death* —death conceived as the final frustration of real values, the evil in which all the evils of the universe (for this theme is cosmic as well as human) come to a head. On the human plane, all moves forward to the point when the Immortal announces to the mortal, "To-day thou shalt be with me in Paradise"; on the cosmic plane all moves forward to the point where the *whole creation* escapes from the bondage of corruption, and the intolerable frustrations attendant upon it, into the liberties of the incorruptible or resurrection life. "Life and immortality were brought to light in the gospel of Jesus Christ." It is a tremendous theme, the full scope and majesty of which seem to have been missed alike by orthodox theology and by modernist reactions.

If there is any member of this audience who expects from me a fully worked out proof of immortality, I must warn him at once that he will be disappointed. It could not be done within my limits. And even if it were done I doubt if it would convince anybody. Besides which it might lead me into some unintentional dishonesty. It might give you the impression that I have a kind of certitude in this matter I do not really possess. Putting aside any reasons we may have from revelation, or from authority, I do not think that the immortality of the soul can be infallibly demonstrated as a philosophical proposition. But I agree with Bishop Butler that probability is the guide of life, and I think that in this matter the probabilities are high. They are high enough to encourage me in regarding myself as an immortal soul, and, what is far more important, in treating my fellow-men as though they were immortal also, which ought to make a great difference in my treatment of them. And yet I would not say that any of us can claim immortality as our birthright, as something to which we are entitled, no matter what use we make of our lives. But I do think that our human personalities are capable of acquiring a value which a just universe would not suffer to be extinguished. I look upon immortality, then, rather as a prize to be won than as a birthright given for nothing. And this, if you will look into the matter, is the doctrine of the New Testament. In the New Testament we are immortal in so far as we becomes the sons and heirs of the immortal God. But none of the writers there represent sonship and heirship to God as a condition into which we are naturally born. The position of sons is one that we have to win, and our immortality follows from that.

That brings me to a point I am anxious to make at this stage. Many writers on our subject have a prejudice against the belief in immortality because they think that it indicates

self-importance on the part of those who hold it.
It is monstrous, or even ridiculous, in their eyes,
that any finite being should consider himself
entitled to live on indefinitely after the term of
his mortal life is ended. But may it not be
pointed out that the question affects not only
the value a man attaches to *himself,* but the
value he attaches to *other people?* I can respect a man who, for philosophic reasons, is indifferent to the prospect of his coming annihilation at death. But I find it much harder to
respect a man who is equally indifferent to the
annihilation of those whom he honours and reverences and loves. Plato brings this out very
beautifully in the *Phaedo.* His arguments for
the immortality of the soul I do not find very
convincing. And yet the *Phaedo* is a perma-
nent contribution to the belief in immortality.
All through that wonderful dialogue Plato
keeps us thinking, not about ourselves and what
is going to happen to us, but about Socrates and
about what is going to happen to that wise and
admirable man. And gradually he works up
to the point, that when Socrates takes the hem-
lock and passes away before our eyes, the
thought that he is done for, that so great and

beautiful a light is gone out for ever, becomes incredible. Here you have a case when the belief in immortality is made to hinge, not on the importance we attach to ourselves, but on the importance we attach to one better than ourselves, whom we honour and love. That surely cannot be regarded as ignoble, or egotistic. And I believe that this feeling has had as much to do in creating our interest in the question as any concern we may have about *our own* fate after death.

When, therefore, I read in the writings of one philosopher that death "doesn't count," or in another that "a wise man thinks of nothing less than he does of death," I always wonder whether it is his own death the philosopher is referring to, or the death of those whom he honours, reverences and loves. These sayings have a very different value according as we take them in the one sense or in the other. When you are thinking of yourself there may be something noble in saying that death doesn't count. But there is nothing noble when we say it of other people—of the countless young men, for example, who perished in the war. On many of the war memorials set up all over the land we may see the words inscribed, "Their name liveth for evermore." But is that literally true? And if so, is it only their *name* that lives? And am I to be accused of self-importance if I insist in believing that *they* live as well as their name? I knew one of the best of men who had definitely abandoned the belief in immortality, and learnt to look forward to his own death with perfect philosophic composure. But when his eldest son was killed in the war that man was broken all to pieces. I think it is out of tragic experiences of that kind, and not from mere self-concern, that the interest men take in this question has mainly arisen.

Indeed, we shall miss the significance of our problem if we regard it as affecting the individual only, as one which each of us asks only about himself. It is a question we ask about others, and this gives it a social significance as well as a private one. The occurrence of death, as the lot sooner or later of every human being, has had a profound influence on all the ties that bind us together in the family and in society, and one may well doubt if any of our deeper affections can be understood at all when death

is left out of account. It affects the value of
the services we render to one another and of
all the improvements we hope to bring about in
the happiness or well-being of the human race.

Whatever other evils we hope to eliminate
from the lot of man it may be taken for granted
that death, as the universal lot of all that live,
will always be left standing. That can never be
abolished, not even by the social revolution.
Well, then, suppose we had it in our power to
reform all the other evils we suffer from and to
make every human being as happy and con-
tented as circumstances permit of—to bring
about the social millennium in fact. What
would be the significance of death in this happy
world we had created? Would people be more
willing to die, and to see their friends die, than
they are now? Or would they be more reluc-
tant to quit so happy a scene and to give up so
desirable an existence? Or think of your social
paradise not in terms of happiness, but in terms
of goodness and of wisdom—a future society
of the good and the wise. The same question
arises. If you think of men and women as
growing in goodness, you think of them as becoming more valuable to one another, more

necessary to one another, more closely bound together by ties of affection and mutual respect. Well, would the partings then be easier or harder than they are now? Would the breaking of the tie be less tragic or more tragic? I have heard the question answered both ways. I have heard it argued that by that time people will have become more philosophic and learnt to take their natural sorrows more calmly and more wisely. I confess the argument does not convince me. People might indeed become calmer and wiser about these things, but would they feel the pang of them any the less for that? Perhaps in their calmness and wisdom the stab might go even deeper than it goes now. You can argue both ways, and I must leave you to answer the question for yourselves. As the world grows better, or happier, does death become less of a frustration or more of a frustration? Whichever answer you give you will at least see what I mean by saying that death has a social significance as well as a private one. It affects the ties that bind us together and the services we render to one another.

Many philosophers seem to have overlooked this side of the question. It was not over-

looked by Plato. In the person of Socrates, as I have said, he puts before us a man of the highest value, an indispensable man, who commands our love and our reverence, and leaves us unable to bear the thought that death has extinguished so admirable a soul. In this way the question of immortality is lifted beyond all personal reference to ourselves, and freed from the taint of selfish desire with which it has been charged.

We are often told that the deepest piety is to accept the will of God in this matter, even though it involves our final extinction at death. "Yea, though he slay me yet will I trust him." I see the truth of that, and feel the force of it. But what if he slay Socrates as well as me? What if all those, the latchet of whose shoes I am not worthy to unloose, are also to be quenched in everlasting night? That I find harder to accept, and I am not sure that piety requires me to accept it.

Those of you who are familiar with the biography of Carlyle will remember how these thoughts were constantly with him during the closing years of his life. "My life now," he said, "has nothing in it but the shadow, sad,

grand and unfathomable, of what is coming—
coming." "God's will there also be supreme."
That was his frame of mind about himself, and
we recognise the deep piety of it. But whenever his thoughts turned to the wife he had
lost—and he was thinking far more about her
than about himself—then he strikes a different
note. That she has gone for ever—simply disappeared into the universal void, gone out in
the everlasting night—this is a thought his mind
refuses to entertain. "At all hours and at all
moments," he writes, "her transfigured spirit
accompanies me, beautiful and sad; lies behind
all thoughts that I have, and even all *talk* that
I carry on." "If we are to meet!" he cries.
"Oh, Almighty Father, if we are; but silence!
silence!"

I confess that in all this I find nothing that
can be properly called a "selfish desire for immortality." Selfish is the last word that should
be applied to it. It betokens a spirit that has
become deeply implicated in the lives of others
and has learned to find its highest values, not in
itself, but in those whom it loves, and in the
reciprocal relations that bind them together.
And that, as I understand it, is the spirit in

which the Christian Religion originally embraced this belief. In the New Testament, the hope of immortality is not grounded on any value we find in ourselves but on the value we find in Another. There is, to begin with, but One Immortal Soul, which becomes the fountain of Immortality to all the other souls that are bound with it in the ties of love and loyalty. It is because Christ lives that we shall live also.

The word with which Carlyle ends the ejaculation I have just quoted is, however, a warning to us. The word is "Silence, silence." I have often felt, and doubtless you also have felt it, that the atmosphere in which the belief in immortality gets its strongest hold upon us, is not the atmosphere of noisy argumentation. In all questions that touch deeply on our spiritual life there is a danger, a very great danger, lest the secondary interests that gather round the argument should obscure the primary interest of the reality we are arguing about. We have all heard of the theologian who became so absorbed in arguing for the existence of God that he forgot to say his prayers. The secondary interest had obscured the primary. That danger is especially great when we are arguing about immortality. For some reason or another—I thing I know what it is, but have no time to go into it now—this subject is peculiarly provocative of a contentious frame of mind. Yet there is no subject in which the contentious spirit is so obstructive—so fatal to our seeing the majesty and significance of what we are talking about. Again we are reminded of Goethe's saying, "The highest cannot be spoken." Obviously there is something here that we cannot speak, and had better not try to speak.

I wish I could keep that disturbing element out of this lecture altogether. But I owe it to you to state some reasons which have led me to think that personal survival after death is not a vain dream and not unworthy of a philosophic mind. They may not convince you. They certainly will not, unless you are able to carry them on in your private meditations, and apply them to many things upon which I cannot touch in this lecture.

My own belief in this matter—so far as it is an argued belief, and it is only so in part—grows out of two others beliefs which I hold

very firmly and think can be made good as doctrines of positive philosophy.

The first is the doctrine, to which I have re-
ferred so often, that the universe is essentially
alive, and not dead—a living being, and not a
lifeless thing.   And the second is the doctrine
that the life of this universe expresses a moral
order, and that its evolution, as we call it, is the
conscious working out of that order into fuller
manifestation and reality.   To go into the reasons for all this is of course impossible.   We can
only glance at each doctrine in turn.

I have said before there are in the last resort
only two doctrines possible as to the nature of
the universe—one holding it to be dead, lifeless,
a mechanism going by a kind of clockwork, and
the other holding it to be essentially alive—and
that not as a cabbage is alive, but as we are,
conscious of itself as a unitary whole and knowing what it is about.   This is the doctrine which
I find myself forced to accept as by far the better alternative of the two.   The saying of the
Gospel—"God is not a God of the dead but of
the living"—I take as covering everything in
space and time, all that the astronomer can tell
us of what goes on in the unimaginable depths

of space, all that the historian can tell us of what has gone on in the unimaginable depths of time. All is alive, and it is *one* life, plainly an immortal life, that animates the whole.

If then there is any sense in which I am one with that universe, any sense in which I am a sharer in its life, then too I become a sharer in its immortality. Life and immortality, not death and mechanism, are the keywords of the real universe, and so far as you and I are true sons of the universe, so far as we reproduce its nature in ourselves, life and immortality are the keywords to our reality also. This, I take it, is the essence of all idealist philosophy. In spite of the many differences among idealists, they all converge towards the proposition that the universe is alive, the embodiment of spirit, or as Goethe says, "the living garment of God." All of them move towards that, and they all move away from the idea that the universe is dead, and that life and consciousness are only exceptional phenomena appearing here and there as circumstances permit. If conscious life is only that, only a by-product of a dead universe, then indeed we might anticipate that this by-product would finish in the same way as it has arisen, that all conscious lives would be refunded into the universal empire of death. But if conscious life is not a mere by-product of that kind, but the essence and reality of the whole, then perhaps we have reason for expecting something else.

When the universe is thought of in this manner—and it is only the accident of our times, and the peculiar mental habits and stock notions we have developed, which make it difficult for us so to think of it—when the universe is thought of in this manner, it ceases to be the mere scene or theatre on which our life is transacted—which is all a dead universe can ever amount to. It becomes essentially a Companion, a living Companion—no new idea, but one which was perfectly familiar to the Stoics and may be found running through all the writings of Marcus Aurelius. That being so, there is now room for raising the question whether you and your Great Companion are not fellow-workers, out for the same thing, whether your purpose and your business are not one with the purpose and business on which the Soul of the World is also intent.

And what are your purpose and business?

To that profound question I can only give, without entering into reasons, the answer which the best thought of the world has always given to it. Your purpose and business are those of a Creator of Values. You are here to add value to the world in which you find yourself. And there lies the point of contact between you and the Great Companion. There is the point where your business and purpose coincide with that of the Soul of the Living Universe. You are fellow-workers in creation. There is a confederacy at that point. And if the Soul of the World asks for your loyalty, may you not expect that it also will be loyal to you, that it will not let you down, that it will not involve either yourself, or any you love, in final frustration? That, I think, is a reasonable question; a question to which we may expect a very definite answer from a reasonable universe. It brings us to our second line of approach.

Again I must leave aside all the reasons, drawn from the deepest experience of life, which have led so many of the best minds, in all ages, to find in that deepest experience the manifestation of a moral order. I must assume that you believe or are willing to believe, with Carlyle, that "the great soul of the world is just."

But now, what do we mean when we say that the world is a moral order? The only answer that will satisfy us was given by Immanuel Kant. A moral world is a world where *persons, individual persons, are treated as ends in themselves,* and not as means or instruments to an end beyond themselves. If I treat you (or you treat me) as merely an instrument, which I may use for furthering some purpose of my own, then, no matter how high that purpose of mine may be, no matter how good that purpose may be, I am not treating you morally but immorally. You, as a person, are an absolute value; but if I make use of you as a means to my own end, however good my end may be, I am making your value relative to mine, I am infringing your absoluteness and I am doing you wrong. My soul is unjust at that point, and nothing that I can say about the goodness of the purpose for which I am sacrificing your value will wipe out the fundamental injustice of my conduct towards you.

We accept all this without murmur when we are thinking about our relationships with one another. No man can claim to be a good man who uses his neighbour as a means or an instrument. That is a commonplace of morality. But what I would now point out is, that exactly the same holds true when we are thinking of our relations to that Being whom Carlyle calls "the great soul of the world"—to whom we commonly give the name of God. If this universe has a soul—and that is what I mean when I say it is not dead but living—and if there is moral order at the base of things—then we are entitled to expect that God treats all souls within that order, yours and mine, not as means or instruments, but as ends in themselves.

Suppose we found it otherwise. Suppose we found that the Great Soul of the World is making use of us as instruments for its own glory, or as pawns in a great game of evolution, or as means to bringing about some "far-off divine event" in which we are not to participate, sacrificing us for that high purpose, and not minding how many of us it sacrificed, then I say that Soul would be doing the very thing which when we do it to one another we recognise as unjust, as the violation of moral order.

On those terms we could not say, "The great soul of the world is just." It would be using us not as ends in ourselves but as means to its own end—the very definition of injustice.

Recall for a moment those well-known lines of George Eliot—"The Choir Invisible." We are to be dissolved into a stream of moral tendency, to live on, after death, "in minds made better by our presence." We live on in the influence for good that our lives exercise on others. But think what that involves. It involves an endless succession of souls, of persons, each of whom exists not for his own end, but that those who come after may be made better, and these aftercomers, too, will find themselves in exactly the same position. The value of A's personality is that it improves the value of B's, and of B's that it improves the value of C's, and so on for ever and ever. A world which used us so would be using us not as ends in ourselves, but as means to an end, and, what is more, to an end that never arrives. It seems to me an arrangement which is quite nonsensical when viewed as a whole, and profoundly unjust when viewed in detail. A world which uses your personality to make me a better man may be acting generously towards me, but it is dealing most unfairly with you. Me it makes the end, you the means. Frankly I would decline, if I had the offer, to be made better on those terms, because I see that it involves a violation of the fundamental principle of a moral world, by using one man as a means to the ends of another, or by sacrificing the interests of one generation in the interests of the generations that are to come. This kind of spectral immortality I find worse than no immortality at all.

We now see what is meant by saying "the great soul of the world is just." It means that in a living universe all souls, all persons, are treated as ends in themselves, and not as mere fodder and fuel for keeping up the process of evolution. That being so, this question immediately arises: Can a universe in which all souls, all persons, are finally extinguished at death be said to treat those persons as ends in themselves? The answer, so far as I am concerned, is No. If we are finally extinguished at death we must be content to regard our personalities as fodder or fuel, as having instrumental value only, but as having no absolute value of their own which would make them ends in themselves. A world in which persons are so treated, as means and not as ends, whatever else it may be, is not moral, and the soul of that world, if it has a soul, is not just. It is true that in certain moods of humility I find it not difficult to regard myself as mere fodder or fuel. But at all times I find it enormously difficult to take that attitude towards others whom I honour and love. I revolt from the thought that the great and good of all ages have lived and died that I, and others like me, may become better men. I look upon it as a foul wrong done to them, and it hurts me to think I am benefited by it. Willing as I may be, in certain moods, to regard myself as fodder and fuel, I cannot so regard Socrates and multitudes of others whom I honour. They were ends in themselves, not mere means to the betterment of others. And as ends in themselves I cannot but believe that the Great Soul of the World looks after them and cares for them and preserves them. "Yea, though he slay me, yet will I trust him." But if he has slain *them,* I can trust him no more.

Least of all can I trust him if he has slain them merely in order that I, and others like me, might enjoy, through their sufferings and death, a fuller life. It is in this way that the belief in Immortality gets bound up with the belief in God. "The Great Soul of the World is just."

THE END